ENCOURAGED

A 21-Day Real Talk Devotional and
45-Day Prompted Bible Journal

Chellbee Johnson

ISBN: 1983851051
ISBN-13: 978-1983851056

ENCOURAGED 45-DAY READING PLAN

Day 1   Isaiah 40

Day 2   Isaiah 43

Day 3   Joshua 1

Day 4   2 Corinthians 1

Day 5   Proverbs 3

Day 6   Isaiah 41

Day 7   2 Timothy 1

Day 8   John 14

Day 9   Psalm 55

Day 10   Psalm 6

Day 11   Psalm 118

Day 12   Psalm 119:169-120:4

Day 13   Psalm 119:105-152

Day 14   Deuteronomy 31

Day 15   Isaiah 26

ENCOURAGED 45-DAY READING PLAN

Day 16   John 16

Day 17   Matthew 11

Day 18   Psalm 31

Day 19   Romans 8

Day 20   Mark 12

Day 21   Psalm 32

Day 22   Ephesians 3:14-21

Day 23   Philippians 4

Day 24   Job 11

Day 25   1 Corinthians 15

Day 26   James 4

Day 27   Psalm 121

Day 28   James 1

Day 29   Psalm 23

Day 30   Genesis 12

ENCOURAGED 45-DAY READING PLAN

Day 31   Isaiah 12

Day 32   Ruth 2

Day 33   1 Peter 5

Day 34   Hebrew 12

Day 35   Philippians 3

Day 36   Hebrew 4

Day 37   Luke 1:26-56

Day 38   Colossians 2

Day 39   Romans 5

Day 40   Ephesians 5

Day 41   Matthew 7

Day 42   Jeremiah 29

Day 43   Romans 15

Day 44   1 Corinthians 13

Day 45   Lamentations 3

How to use the Journal

There are many approaches to studying the bible from Bible art, group Bible studies, to independent reading. Your experience with the Bible is whatever you make of it. The most important thing about studying the bible is getting started and sticking with it.

Praise and worship are great but creating a one on one relationship with God is amazing. By committing to reading the Bible daily you gain a deeper understanding and connection to the word.

No matter where you are on your spiritual journey you don't need much for this Bible Journaling techniques to work for you. Make sure you choose a Bible reading version that is easy to read. A study bible is a great option if you want access to reference notes to gain a better understanding.

Make the commitment to yourself that bible journaling will be a part of your daily routine. Plan for at least 15-30 minutes of quiet time. Start journaling every day first thing in the morning. Grab a hot cup and get cozy with your bible and journal.

Ultimately this technique is the simplest way I have found to study the Bible. The purpose of bible journaling is not to be an expert. But to try to gain a better understanding of the word for yourself. Reading the Bible is an opportunity to learn something new about the world, yourself, and life lessons.

Bible Journaling

I Heard Write down the verse (s) that speak to you.

Thank You For What revelation did you have that made you thankful.

I Observed What were the major occurrences, what stood out, and what was the sentiments.

I Learned What lessons did you learn and how did it make you feel? How does what you read apply to your life?

I Pray What do you want to tell God. What do you need his help with.

Encouraged: A 21-Day Real Talk Devotional and 45-Day Prompted Bible Journal

Day One Devotional

"But those who hope in the Lord will renew their strength. They will soar on wings like eagles; they will run and not grow weary, they will walk and not be faint."

-Isaiah 40:31 NIV

How often have you thought there is just no way, I can do this. Like Lord I can't do this thing on my own. I need your help and I need it right now. I had this moment more times than I'd like to admit. I know there is nothing wrong with seeking God help. But it can be demoralizing to come to God cowering like a dog with my tail in between my legs.

Ever since I took the leap and left my job, I feel like I'm running a 10k marathon that I didn't sign up or train for. Have you ever made a decision with such confidence and later realized you're in way over your head. While let me just say if life is a marathon, then I'm wheezing, dizzy, and weak.

You try to remind yourself that life is a journey and not a

destination. Slow and steady will win the race. Then you look around and you see everyone speeding pass you. So you try to catch up and before you know it, you've passed out.

You open your eyes only to realize everyone is still running and now there stepping over you. Feeling like a complete idiot, you pick yourself up. You realize that you're going to either give up or keep going. And if you're going to continue in this race then you have to approach it differently this time.

I'm embarrassed to admit how long it took me to realized I can't run this marathon called life without God. I would always start the race with the right intentions. But somewhere along the way I'd get distracted by all the people passing me by, what was happening on the sideline, or simply pass out from exhaustion. I was too stubborn or independent to recognize that God is my strength.

Sometimes failure can act as a defining moment in your faith. Failure brings you to a familiar crossroad where you have to decide if you are going to lean on your own wisdom or seek God's wisdom whole-heartedly. I'm so thankful I choose God's wisdom and realized I don't know anything.

Now when I want to give up, I take a deep breath, rest, and ask God for the strength and guidance to go forward. We may not know what is ahead of us but we must believe that God has already given us everything we need to win. In those moments when you find yourself feeling weak remember to have faith in God's ability to provide and be patience because His timing is perfect.

Day One Journal

◊ Describe a time when God showed you favored and you felt as though you didn't deserve it.

◊ In what ways do you feel God has given you strength when you were weary?

◊ In what aspect of your life do you need to wait on the Lord and how do you plan to do so?

_____

_____

_____

_____

_____

_____

_____

_____

_____

_____

_____

_____

_____

_____

Bible Journal　　　　　*Isaiah* 40　　　　　Date _____

I *Thank* You for

I *Heard* You _____

_____

_____

_____

_____

I *Observed*

I *Learned* _____

_____

_____

_____

_____

I *Pray*

Day Two Journal

◊ Describe a time when you felt you were going through your own personal hell. How did you make it through? Did you feel alone?

◊ When you made it onto the other side (and overcame the hell). At what point did you realize God was with you?

_____

_____

_____

_____

_____

_____

_____

_____

_____

_____

_____

_____

_____

_____

_____

_____

_____

_____

_____

_____

_____

_____

_____

_____

_____

_____

_____

_____

_____

_____

_____

_____

_____

_____

_____

_____

_____

_____

Bible Journal   Isaiah 43   Date _____

I Thank You for

I Heard You _____
_____
_____
_____
_____
_____

I Observed

I Learned _____
_____
_____
_____
_____

I Pray

Day Three Devotional

"Have I not commanded you? Be strong and courageous. Do not be afraid; do not be discouraged, for the Lord your God will be with you wherever you go."

- Joshua 1:9 NIV

Can you imagine what must have been going through Joshua's mind after hearing this word? Lord you want me to do what? Wait... I don't think I heard you right. My mind must, be playing tricks on me. Me, little old' me...

Two months before I had planned to leave my job, I heard God tell me to quit it was distinct and loud. You would think I would have listened, after all, I was planning to quit anyways right. I didn't listen because at the time it didn't match the plan I had for myself.

I quickly lived to regret that decision. All the while trying to convince myself there was no way I could have heard Him right. He knew what was coming. Unfortunately, I'm sure He knew I would be too afraid and stubborn to listen to Him.

Sometimes we allow our fear and self- doubt to stops us

from following the path that God has set out for us. We feel were not ready, were not worthy, or were distracted. That little old' me moment taught me that the way I see myself is not the way God sees me.

Back then, I could have never imagined I would be who I am today. I have grown so much mentally and spiritually in ways that I never knew were possible.

Sometimes we allow other people to define who we are a nd what we are capable of. We limit ourselves. Constantly s hrinking and hiding, all the while too afraid to acknowledge the plan God has for our lives.

I know it's easy to be normal and follow the crowd. But i t takes courage to stand on God's promises the way Joshua did. God created us to rule over this earth, not to hide in it. Be willing and ready to listen and walk according to the tru th that is written in His word.

God doesn't make mistakes. He created you to be strong , courageous, and successful. He has provided you with eve rything you need to win in His word. You just need to read, meditate, believe, pray, and live by it. Commit to getting to know the word and you will find yourself.

Day Three Journal

◊ What can you do to focus on who God says you are instead of what people say you are?

◊ How can you exhibit courage like Joshua in your life right now?

_____

_____

_____

_____

_____

_____

_____

_____

_____

_____

_____

_____

_____

_____

_____

Bible Journal   *Joshua* 1   Date _____

I *Thank* You for

I *Heard* You _____

_____

_____

_____

_____

I *Observed*

I *Learned* _____

_____

_____

_____

_____

I *Pray*

Day Four Journal

◊ Reflect on a time when someone's testimony touched you. Why did their testimony affect you and how did it change you?

◊ How can sharing your testimony inspire someone around you?

_____

_____

_____

_____

_____

_____

_____

_____

_____

_____

_____

_____

_____

_____

_____

_____

_____

_____

_____

_____

_____

_____

_____

_____

_____

_____

_____

_____

_____

_____

_____

_____

_____

_____

_____

_____

_____

_____

_____

Bible Journal   *2 Corinthians* 1   Date _____

I *Thank* You for

I *Heard* You _____

_____

_____

_____

_____

_____

I *Observed*

I *Learned* _____

_____

_____

_____

_____

_____

I *Pray*

Day Five Devotional

"Trust in the Lord with all your heart and lean not on your own understanding; in all your ways submit to him, and he will make your paths straight."

- Proverb 3:5-6 NIV

Do you ever get caught up in your own hype? Do you have a big ego? Are you feeling yourself? It's ok to be honest. I think we all have a tendency to let compliments and success go to our heads.

Last year after I released my first book I was definitely feeling myself. My chest was all puffed out and I didn't know enough about the word just yet to understand I hadn't made it yet. I had started the celebration prematurely.

I don't know about you but when I get a small bit of momentum I allow it to catapult me into full on dream mode. Don't get me wrong 2017 was good to me. But I started it off with a crazy long list of goals that had less to do with God and more to do with boosting my ego.

I attempted to charge forward doing everything in my

power to make them a reality. I was ready and willing to knock people down, ignore my surrounding, and shut out anything that didn't agree with my goals. Let's just say tunnel vision can be our downfall.

I was blindly forging ahead with no concern for anyone else but myself. Don't get me wrong I continued to read the word and try to be a good person. But I still wasn't focused on what was truly important. God's word.

It wasn't until my business hit a wall that I realized I still had a long ways to go in terms of spiritual growth. Discouraged I refocused, prayed, and continued to read the Bible. Eventually I realized we go through these seasons because we don't wake up ready to walk into our season of prosperity.

I know now that I am in my season of waiting. This season is helping me to strengthen my faith, silence my own wants and desire, and become a better servant. I thankful for so many reasons that I didn't accomplish several of my 2017 goals, because they were misguided.

Our knowledge can only take us so far in this life. If we silence ourselves for long, enough we'll begin to recognize and surrender to God's wisdom and guidance. When we stop looking at problems with our perspective and begin to seek God, we find peace.

Submit to His perfect timing, pray continuously, and have faith that God can do all things. Acknowledge we are nothing and know nothing without Him. Resist the urge to have a big ego. Because all good things are from God.

Day Five Journal

◊ How can trusting the Lord with all your heart make life easier?

◊ Reflect on a time when you made a decision based on your own wisdom. How did things turn out, did they work out or did they create an unnecessary mess?

_____

_____

_____

_____

_____

_____

_____

_____

_____

_____

_____

_____

_____

_____

_____

_____

_____

Bible Journal   *Proverbs* 3   Date _____

I *Thank* You for

I *Heard* You _____

_____

_____

_____

_____

_____

I *Observed*

I *Learned* _____

_____

_____

_____

_____

I *Pray*

Day Six Journal

◊ Reflect on a time when God shielded you from something or someone that was trying to harm you.

◊ Write a prayer asking God for strength during times of uncertainty or fear.

_____

_____

_____

_____

_____

_____

_____

_____

_____

_____

_____

_____

_____

_____

_____

_____

_____

_____

_____

_____

_____

_____

_____

_____

_____

_____

_____

_____

_____

_____

_____

_____

_____

_____

_____

_____

_____

_____

_____

_____

_____

Bible Journal Isaiah 41 Date _____

I Thank You for

I Heard You _____

_____

_____

_____

_____

_____

I Observed

I Learned _____

_____

_____

_____

_____

_____

I Pray

Day Seven Devotional

"For the Spirit God gave us does not make us timid, but gives us power, love and self-discipline."

- 2 Timothy 1:7 NIV

Don't get me wrong, I enjoy a good Monday motivation quote. I think it is a great way to start your week, stay positive, and stay motivated. But as I've grown spiritually I began to notice the disconnect between Monday motivation and faith. I'm not saying Monday motivation has to be a bible verse in order to be meaningful.

What I am saying is when I was in the Monday motivation mindset there wasn't much room for God. The Monday motivation mindset lends itself to the thought that it's all about you. You can do it alone.

I think sometimes as Christians we find it easier to say, "You got this, girl" instead of saying "Jesus is holding your hand" or "Let us pray." You have to be careful about what you consume and what you allow yourself to believe. If you believe, that God is in control and Jesus is your Lord and Savior.

Then you have to be willing to say that and you need to say that proudly. Believe me I know it's not easy. When I began to talk about my faith openly pretty much everyone in my life thought I was crazy. It was like they thought I joined a cult or something. I will be the first to admit it made me self-conscious but I wasn't going to back down.

Don't let society force you to conform into a motivation mindset when you really are a Jesus girl. I'm not saying stop strangers on the street and proclaim your love for Christ. But I am saying don't let anyone make you feel ashamed to say "Praise Jesus".

We have to give ourselves back to God and acknowledge we are His. You will never experience the fullness of this life if you're afraid to acknowledge who God is in your life. The greatest gift we will ever receive is allowing Him to work through us.

Day Seven Journal

◊ How can you be bold in your faith today?
◊ How are you and will you preserve the word of God in your heart?

_____

_____

_____

_____

_____

_____

_____

_____

_____

_____

_____

_____

_____

_____

_____

_____

_____

_____

_____

_____

_____

_____

_____

_____

_____

_____

_____

_____

_____

_____

_____

_____

_____

_____

_____

_____

_____

_____

Bible Journal   *2 Timothy* 1   Date _____

I *Thank* You for

I *Heard* You _____

_____

_____

_____

_____

_____

I *Observed*

I *Learned* _____

_____

_____

_____

_____

_____

I *Pray*

Day Eight Journal

◊ Write down five things that currently have you worried.

◊ Turn your worries into prayers! Write down prayers giving those worries over to Jesus. Trust that he is with you, "Peace I leave with you."

_____

_____

_____

_____

_____

_____

_____

_____

_____

_____

_____

_____

_____

_____

Bible Journal   John 14   Date _____

I Thank You for

I Heard You _____

_____

_____

_____

_____

_____

I Observed

I Learned _____

_____

_____

_____

_____

_____

I Pray

Day Nine Devotional

>>———————►

"Cast your cares on the Lord and he will sustain you; he will never let the righteous be shaken."

- Psalm 55:22 NIV

We have all experienced haters rather it was at your high school, workplace, church, or social media. At some point for some reason, we will all experience what it feels like to be disliked. Maybe they disliked you for no fault of your own or because of a past disagreement.

No matter the reason, it's not a pleasant feeling to be disliked. I never thought of myself as someone who needed to be liked by others. I more of a you can take me or leave me kind of person.

But, there are times when no matter what your attitude is ignoring a hater is hard to do. During my corporate America stint, I got along great with everyone. We had great team chemistry, except there was this one woman.

She would smile in everyone's face but as soon as you would turn around it was a different story. Slowly but surely everyone began to keep their distance from her. In hopes of calming, the flames on the fire but it had the opposite effect. Very quickly, the office became a toxic minefield that no one felt safe in.

Our team morale quickly faded, chemistry dimmed, smiles diminished, and attitudes became less than pleasant. One person managed to change the attitudes of an entire group of people. Looking back on that experience it saddens me that we allowed one person to deterrent our happiness.

We'll never know what motivates someone to hate or dislike us. But I do know that you can't allow how someone else feels about you to stop you from being yourself. Love truly is the only thing that can conquer hate.

Think about it if you choose to be hateful in return who wins. Believe me it's not you. I think about how much energy and joy I let someone steal from me. Then I think about how much time I wasted talking about it with friends and family allowing myself to stay in that mindset even outside of work.

Hatred is toxic. You have to make the decision not to give it power. Now when I get a crazy emails, comments, or message I do not tell others about it. You have to choose to stop breathing life into negativity.

Pray for those who try to come against you. I know it hard and the last thing you probably want to do. But let me tell you God is your best weapon against an enemy. Only He can see what's in our hearts and help turn things around.

Day Nine Journal

◊ What are three ways you can overcome negativity?

◊ Write down an affirmation that you can say to yourself to handle negativity.

_____

_____

_____

_____

_____

_____

_____

_____

_____

_____

_____

_____

_____

_____

_____

_____

_____

_____

_____

_____

_____

_____

_____

_____

_____

_____

_____

_____

_____

_____

_____

_____

_____

_____

_____

_____

_____

Bible Journal   Psalm 55   Date _____

I Thank You for

I Heard You _____
_____
_____
_____
_____
_____

I Observed

I Learned _____
_____
_____
_____
_____

I Pray

Day Ten Journal

◊ Write down five mistakes you have made that you are still carrying with you right now.

◊ Using that list, write down your confessions and prayers for forgiveness.

_____

_____

_____

_____

_____

_____

_____

_____

_____

_____

_____

_____

_____

_____

_____

_____

_____

_____

Bible Journal   Psalm 6   Date _____

I Thank You for

I Heard You _____

_____

_____

_____

_____

_____

I Observed

I Learned _____

_____

_____

_____

_____

I Pray

Day Eleven Devotional

"The Lord is my strength and my defense; he has become my salvation."

- Psalm 118:14 NIV

Have you ever been so weary and weak that you could not even come to battle on your own behalf? May be you were physically, mentally, or emotionally unable to stand up for yourself in that moment. But somehow some way without you uttering a word or making a move God intervened on your behalf.

In July of 2016, God did just that for me without my knowledge. It was the weekend and my husband had just left for work. I was lounging in bed when I got the urge to use the bathroom, so I went but nothing came out. I got back in bed and decided to take a nap.

I had not been lying for long before I woke up with this pain in my stomach. So I switched from lying on my back to lying on my side. Within moments I again, felt the urge to go to the bathroom. So I attempted to sit up but the pain in my stomach intensified.

I laid back down and called my husband. He came home and tried to help me out of the bed. But I immediately slumped over in pain. When I tried to stand, it felt as though my entire insides were falling to the ground. The pain was gut wrenching.

We went to the emergency room. They performed a CT scan and found internal bleeding. After several test, pain medication, and a hospital transfer. The best the doctors could hypothesis was that maybe an ovarian cyst had burst.

I called my job to let them know I would not be in and that I didn't know when I would be in again. I returned home after 3 days and went back to work a week later. When I returned a close coworker of mine let me know that another one of our coworker (the woman with the toxic energy) mentioned wanting to visit me at the hospital. Thankfully, my friend was able to convince her that it wasn't a good idea.

If you ask me that was nothing short of Divine intervention. This woman had made my work life a living hell. I couldn't believe she had the audacity to think I would want her to visit me in the hospital. Especially when we had never spent time outside of work together.

God knew the power I had given this woman over my joy. I am so thankful that when I was at my lowest, He protected me. He knew that the last thing I needed was to be forced to interact with someone who I felt didn't care about me.

In that moment, I needed a shield. God sent it in His perfect timing. God is stronger than any human power. Even when we are unable to stand in our own defense God will be there to send us help when we are in need.

Day Eleven Journal

◊ What obstacles are you currently battling that you need God's strength to overcome?

◊ What are you going to do to show God that you trust Him to be your defense?

_____

_____

_____

_____

_____

_____

_____

_____

_____

_____

_____

_____

_____

_____

_____

Bible Journal   *Psalm* 118   Date

I *Thank* You for

I *Heard* You _____

_____

_____

_____

_____

I *Observed*

I *Learned* _____

_____

_____

_____

_____

I *Pray*

Day Twelve Journal

◊ In what way can you seek the Lord?

◊ How can you show the Lord you desire Him?

◊ What are the 10 commandments?

_____

_____

_____

_____

_____

_____

_____

_____

_____

_____

_____

_____

_____

_____

_____

_____

_____

Bible Journal   Psalm 119:169-120:4   Date _____

I Thank You for

I Heard You _____

_____

_____

_____

_____

_____

I Observed

I Learned _____

_____

_____

_____

_____

_____

I Pray

Day Thirteen Devotional

>———————►

"You are my refuge and my shield; I have put my hope in your word. Away from me, you evildoers, that I may keep the commands of my God!"

- Psalm 119:114-115 NIV

When I first got the idea to be a faith blogger I thought, there is no way that this will work. I had just begun to read the Bible. I wasn't in the church. I felt like there was too much that I didn't know about Christ, the Lord, and the Word.

I couldn't relate to a lot of the blogs I came across. Because frankly their story, knowledge, or resources didn't fit my needs. We are all starting at different paths and places within our spiritual journey. I needed someone who was going to speak to me on the level I am at right now.

I honestly thought I couldn't possibly add to the conversation. Then I thought well maybe there were people out there like me. Who wanted to strengthen their relationship with God but don't know where to start. So I prayed about it. In time, I got up the courage to share faith post on my blog.

In time, I heard from so many people who related to my journey. I was so thankful just to be a help. But eventually I did meet some negative point of views. Primarily from people who felt there are certain things every 'beginner Christian knows', whatever that means.

Last time I checked there is no universal Dummies Guide that all Christians are required to read. Nevertheless, that experience made me realize there is no amount of church attendance, bible study, or prayer that will make us perfect as Christian. Christians can be so critical of ourselves and others. Often we fail to recognize that God love us all the same and His love for us is continuous.

God doesn't reserve His love for us until were perfect. He accepts us and loves us as we are today. All He asks is that we allow Him into our lives with open arms accepting Christ as our Savior and God as our Lord.

I believe that if we give ourselves and everything we love back to Christ as a living sacrifice. He will make us the kinds of people He wants us to be. The person you aspire to be.

- He will cleanse us.
- He will protect us.
- He will deliver us from evil
- He will make crooked path straight.
- He will bring us joy.
- He will give us hope.
- He will give us eternal life.

Day Thirteen Journal

◊ What are you doing to place your hopes in the Word of God?
◊ How can you keep God's commandments in your heart?
◊ Write a prayer asking for God's protection.

_____

_____

_____

_____

_____

_____

_____

_____

_____

_____

_____

_____

_____

_____

_____

_____

Bible Journal   Psalm 119:105-152   Date _____

I Thank You for

I Heard You _____

_____

_____

_____

_____

I Observed

I Learned _____

_____

_____

_____

_____

I Pray

Day Fourteen Journal

◊ How can you be courageous even when you have made a mistake or sinned?

◊ Why do you think God said be "strong and courageous" even though He knew the people would sin once they got to the Promised Land (over the Jordan)?

_____

_____

_____

_____

_____

_____

_____

_____

_____

_____

_____

_____

_____

_____

_____

_____

_____

Encouraged: A 21-Day Real Talk Devotional and 45-Day Prompted Bible Journal

Bible Journal   Deuteronomy 31   Date _____

I Thank You for

I Heard You _____

_____

_____

_____

_____

_____

I Observed

I Learned _____

_____

_____

_____

_____

I Pray

Day Fifteen Devotional

"You will keep in perfect peace those whose minds are steadfast, because they trust in you."

- Isaiah 26:3 NIV

In college, I was very ambitious, hardworking, strong minded, and strong willed. I ran to the beat of my own drum. I paved my own path. I was fiercely reliant on myself. Let me tell it I was good to go in every aspect of life.

Like most ambitious young people, I believed that if I worked hard, got my education, and gained experience in my field I could do anything. Boy was I wrong. But back then you couldn't tell me nothing. I thought I knew it all and had it all together. I was going to be educated, attractive, stylish, connected, and climbing up that corporate ladder with my eyes closed.

Although I knew who God was, I didn't trust God. I couldn't even begin to understand what it meant to trust in God plan for you. I thought being a believer was enough. I didn't recognize I was only a believer on my own terms.

Believing that God is real and developing a relationship with Him are two different things entirely, which I soon found out.

If you're too proud, ignorant, or self-reliant you'll probably find out the hard way like I did. That if you don't humble yourself then God will humble you. When my corporate dreams became a nightmare I realized the only thing I had left was God.

Feeling alone lost, and like I didn't have a friend in the world. I came to Him begging that He would help me turn my life around. In that, moment I realized everything that I thought was important was actually meaningless without God in the picture.

Sometime failure places you on the path you need to be in, in order to seek God's fulfillment instead of your own. Failure made me want to know who God really is. I wanted Him. I needed Him. But most of all I finally realized I was nothing without Him. I stopped relying on my own knowledge and began to Trust God.

Day Fifteen Journal

◊ In what ways can you show God you trust Him?

◊ Describe what peace means for you and your life. What does it look like?

_____

_____

_____

_____

_____

_____

_____

_____

_____

_____

_____

_____

_____

_____

_____

_____

_____

Bible Journal   Isaiah 26   Date _____

I Thank You for

I Heard You _____
_____
_____
_____
_____
_____

I Observed

I Learned _____
_____
_____
_____
_____

I Pray

Day Sixteen Journal

◊ What does "I have overcome the world" mean to you?
◊ Based on what you read, what does peace mean in the scriptural context?
◊ How does it make you feel to know Jesus left you with peace?

_____

_____

_____

_____

_____

_____

_____

_____

_____

_____

_____

_____

_____

_____

_____

_____

_____

Bible Journal   John 16   Date _____

I Thank You for

I Heard You _____
_____
_____
_____
_____
_____

I Observed

I Learned _____
_____
_____
_____
_____

I Pray

Day Seventeen Devotional

"Come to me, all you who are weary and burdened, and I will give you rest."

- Matthew 11:28 NIV

Maybe it's just me but I've always thought of myself as someone who is deserving of salvation. No I'm not perfect I have definitely made my fair share of mistakes and sinned. But my past never caused me to believe I was unworthy of God's love or salvation.

As I've began to grow spiritually over the last two years I have noticed an odd pattern with my friends that grew up in the church. First I want to preface this by saying church very well may have nothing to do with it, there experience is likely more a reflection of their interpretation of the word, experience, or perspective. Nevertheless, they are very critical of themselves spiritually.

They often say things like:
- I just feel like I have done enough to get to heaven.
- I do not feel worthy of His love.
- I've sinned the same sin repeatedly and I just don't

see how He could forgive me.

Personally, I could never relate to their thought process. I often wonder if it's because I've only spent about a year in church my entire life. So maybe I have less biblical teachings to draw on than they do. On the other hand, I've wondered if my Bible reading thus far has shaped me to see Christianity, God, and Christ differently.

Either way, I just don't know that God they speak of. I don't see Him that way. But I recognize that we all can learn different things from the same passage or sermon. Our different backgrounds, experience, and lifestyles shape our perspective drastically.

Although I can't understand how we share the same fundamental beliefs but seem to be on different planets when it comes to salvation. This verse to me confirms there is nothing we as Christian have to do to receive salvation besides trust in Jesus and Lord God. If you do that then forgiveness and eternal life is for you.

No matter what you've done or been through you can and will be forgiven. Forgiveness is an option for all of us because God is not human. He is not like us. He is not keeping a scorecard. He is not a three strikes and you're out kind of God. Aren't we all so thankful for that.

Day Seventeen Journal

◊ How can you find rest in Christ today?

◊ What does believing in Christ mean to you?

_____

_____

_____

_____

_____

_____

_____

_____

_____

_____

_____

_____

_____

_____

_____

_____

_____

_____

_____

Bible Journal   Matthew 11   Date _____

I Thank You for

I Heard You _____

_____

_____

_____

_____

_____

I Observed

I Learned _____

_____

_____

_____

_____

I Pray

Day Eighteen Journal

◊ Describe a time when you felt as though the world was against you. How did you feel? How did you overcome it?

◊ How can you wait on the Lord?

_____

_____

_____

_____

_____

_____

_____

_____

_____

_____

_____

_____

_____

_____

_____

_____

_____

_____

_____

_____

_____

_____

_____

_____

_____

_____

_____

_____

_____

_____

_____

_____

_____

_____

_____

_____

_____

_____

Bible Journal   *Psalm* 31   Date _____

I *Thank* You for

I *Heard* You _____

_____

_____

_____

_____

_____

I *Observed*

I *Learned* _____

_____

_____

_____

_____

_____

I *Pray*

Day Nineteen Devotional

"What, then, shall we say in response to these things? If God is for us, who can be against us?"

- Romans 8:31 NIV

I haven't talked much about this, but this is my second pregnancy. When my husband and I decided to have kids it was kind of a big deal. We had always said if it happened, it happened.

We weren't going to try and we weren't really interested in being parents. But one day out of the clear blue sky while I was driving to the grocery store God turned my heart around. Literally, in seconds I knew in my hearts that we should be parents. So I talked to my husband and we decided to try.

We got pregnant immediately. I literally missed my next period. We were so excited. To be honest we were busting at the seams to share the news. But I knew that miscarriage was a possibility so I told my husband we should wait. And so we did.

We shared the news with our family when we were about 8 weeks. The next day after sharing our big news, I noticed that I was spotting. Initially I was nervous but I wasn't ready to give into the idea that having a baby wasn't going to happen.

At the time, I was in between doctors and could not get in to see my new doctor. So after about 3 days of phone tag and talking to our new doctor's nurse we went to the ER. I swear this was the longest ER wait of my life.

The ER was slow but it was taking forever to be seen by anyone. We eventually had an ultrasound performed and the ultrasound tech keep asking me how far along I was. Finally, she just said it, if I was 8 weeks there should be something in there. We had miscarried (in the form of a blighted ovum).

We were devastated. I don't know what was worst the physical pain of miscarrying or having to share the news with our family. After that experience we we're less than thrilled about trying again. But of course neither of us would say it that to each other.

We literally had intercourse once after the miscarriage. Neither of us thought much about it. But by July we're pregnant again with baby Rose. Mind you, our miscarriage was confirmed at the beginning of June. Needless to say, when I told my husband we were pregnant again he literally didn't believe me.

Within almost a month, God had turned around our suffering. Finding out we were pregnant again made that gut wrenching lost worth it. I could have never imagined that our rainbow would appear so quickly after the storm.
Early on I had to recognize that we still weren't out of the dark. I prayed repeatedly that we would get the chance to be parents to baby Rose.

All the while still surrendering to God will, which wasn't always easy. But I had to remind myself that whatever God has for me is for me.

Surrendering to God plan is never easy. In the end, you have to believe and trust that God only wants good things for you. When you're suffering the best thing you can do is surrender to God's will and remember he only wants good things for you.

Day Nineteen Journal

◊ What does it mean to you to be more than a conqueror?

◊ How does that make you feel to know that nothing can separate you from God's love?

_____

_____

_____

_____

_____

_____

_____

_____

_____

_____

_____

_____

_____

_____

_____

_____

_____

_____

_____

Bible Journal   *Romans* 8   Date _____

I *Thank* You for

I *Heard* You _____

_____

_____

_____

_____

I *Observed*

I *Learned* _____

_____

_____

_____

_____

I *Pray*

Day Twenty Journal

◊ Why do you think this is the greatest commandment?

◊ How can you honor this commandment today?

_____

_____

_____

_____

_____

_____

_____

_____

_____

_____

_____

_____

_____

_____

_____

_____

_____

_____

_____

_____

_____

_____

_____

_____

_____

_____

_____

_____

_____

_____

_____

_____

_____

_____

_____

_____

_____

_____

_____

Bible Journal　　　　Mark 12　　　　Date _____

I Thank You for

I Heard You _____

_____

_____

_____

_____

_____

I Observed

I Learned _____

_____

_____

_____

_____

_____

I Pray

Day Twenty-One Devotional

"I will instruct you and teach you in the way you should go;
I will counsel you with my loving eye on you."

- Psalm 32:8 NIV

I think sometimes as Christian we think we have to be perfect examples. We think that God expects us not to make mistakes. We hold ourselves to these unrealistic expectations. Failing to recognize that we are human beings and not God or Christ.

One of the sayings I have come to live by as a new Christian is to allow my walk to speak for me. I intentionally try not to speak about the type of Christian I am working to be. Because I know that what I believe today may very well change tomorrow.

The person I was one year ago is so different from who I am today. Therefore, I expect that I will go through similar changes in my Christian journey. As I learn more about the Word and deepen my relationship with Christ and our Lord my values may very well change.

But that's ok. People change. We grow. We learn new

things. We overcome our circumstances. And we evolve.

I decided early on that I'm not going to be embarrassed about my past. I'm not going to hide from it. Or allow anyone to make me feel as though I am less than for not being who they feel I should have been in the past because I'm a Christian.

In my heart, I strongly believe it doesn't matter if you were saved as a child, teenager, adult, or senior God loves us all the same.

No one is any better than anyone else. We are all God's people. Therefore, we all have our own journey to embark on toward finding God.

We only hurt ourselves by hiding from our past. Or shaming others because we feel they don't lead the type of life we see fit for Christians. No one is without sin. I don't care how far you've come in your journey no one is perfect.

If we would stop focusing on perfection and creating this Christian persona. And instead, choose to focus on allowing the Lord to teach us. We would find the freedom we all desire and need to grow.

Day Twenty-One Journal

◊ How can you seek God's guidance today?

◊ Write a prayer, thanking God that he does not require you to be perfect but to simply be a believer.

_____

_____

_____

_____

_____

_____

_____

_____

_____

_____

_____

_____

_____

_____

_____

_____

_____

_____

_____

_____

_____

_____

_____

_____

_____

_____

_____

_____

_____

_____

_____

_____

_____

_____

_____

_____

_____

_____

_____

_____

_____

_____

Bible Journal   *Psalm* 32   Date _____

I *Thank* You for

I *Heard* You _____

_____

_____

_____

_____

_____

I *Observed*

I *Learned* _____

_____

_____

_____

_____

_____

I *Pray*

Day Twenty-Two Journal

◊   What is the Holy Spirit and what is its purpose?

◊   What can you do to carry Christ in your heart?

_____

_____

_____

_____

_____

_____

_____

_____

_____

_____

_____

_____

_____

_____

_____

_____

_____

Bible Journal   Ephesians 3:14-21   Date _____

I Thank You for

I Heard You _____
_____
_____
_____
_____
_____

I Observed

I Learned _____
_____
_____
_____
_____
_____

I Pray

Day Twenty-Three Devotional

"I can do all things through him who strengthens me."
- Philippians 4:13 NIV

This maybe taboo to say but I have yet to be considered a full time blogger. Yes, my blog and audience has grown significantly. Which I'm truly thankful for. But the reality is audience size doesn't equal money in the bank as a blogger.

Making money online is not easy and doesn't happens overnight. At least it hasn't for me. Just like quitting, your job doesn't mean you'll be happy.

Believe me when I say that throughout this journey I have wanted to give up so many times. I have made several back up plans and looked into ton of career options. Eventually I would always come back to the same place. Usually after each door was shut in my face, I'd realize that wasn't what God had planned for me.

Eventually I stop acting out long enough to realize I needed to focus. Focus on being content and happy with what I had right now. It took time for me to truly realized and understand the important of Now. I can't expect God to bless me with more when I don't acknowledge Him for what he has already given me.

I am so thankful that I have a great support system. There is no way I would still be doing this without the support of my husband and family. Once I began focus on what I had, relevant opportunities and the appropriate people began to cross my path.

I realized the more time I spent focused on God and being a good servant. Instead of looking for my next check, that's when the tides began to change. I don't expect to be an overnight success because I know I will not overnight become the perfect servant.

I spend most of my energy now on expressing my gratitude. I try to stay focused on Gods way and not my own. But most of all I'm willing to wait on God to lead the way.

Trusting God is also about us allowing him to use and work through us. Thinking of God first and yourself last. When you trust God you not only believe in his word but you exercise obedience.

Day Twenty-Three Journal

◊   What can you do to be content in any circumstance?
◊   How can you exercise obedient as a servant of God today?

_____

_____

_____

_____

_____

_____

_____

_____

_____

_____

_____

_____

_____

_____

_____

_____

_____

_____

Bible Journal   *Philippians* 4   Date _____

I *Thank* You for

I *Heard* You _____

_____

_____

_____

_____

I *Observed*

I *Learned* _____

_____

_____

_____

_____

I *Pray*

Day Twenty-Four Journal

◊ Sometimes our focus is solely on doing things and as a result, we fail to come to God in prayer and repentance. What systems can you put into practice in your life to ensure that God's way prevails?

◊ Write a prayer asking the Lord to "prepare your heart."

_____

_____

_____

_____

_____

_____

_____

_____

_____

_____

_____

_____

_____

_____

_____

_____

Bible Journal   Job 11   Date _____

I Thank You for

I Heard You _____
_____
_____
_____
_____
_____

I Observed

I Learned _____
_____
_____
_____
_____
_____

I Pray

Day Twenty-Five Devotional

"Therefore, my dear brothers and sisters, stand firm. Let nothing move you. Always give yourselves fully to the work of the Lord, because you know that your labor in the Lord is not in vain."

- 1 Corinthian 15:58 NIV

When I first began my spiritual journey, I didn't understand the important of various people sharing the word. I couldn't appreciate why there were so many people speaking about spirituality. I would see the long list of teachers, preachers, devotionals, books, journals, blogs, and resources and I would think what is the point of it all.

Can't we all just read the Bible and have the same experience. Wouldn't it make more sense for us all to just go to the source. But boy was I wrong and for more reasons than one.

Over time, I began to understand that our ability to digest information is shaped by their personal experiences. Which is why you can put 100 people in one room for a sermon and none of them will have the same reaction or experience. Additionally, when we're learning new information it important for us to have resources we trust.

To effectively grow Gods Kingdom, we need as many people and resources as possible. People tend to trust someone who looks like us, has had similar experiences as us, or whom we consider an expert. In order to grow God's Kingdom we need as many people possible whom are willing to share their experience and knowledge.

We all have to do our part to contribute to the work of the Lord. If you've ever considered sharing your testimony but were discouraged. Please recognize there is always someone who could benefit from your voice and your story.

Even if you just touch one person, you could have an everlasting impact on the growth of God's kingdom. We all have to do as much as we can, with what we have. Be a voice for His kingdom. Don't let anyone silence your voice.

I think it makes God proud to see so many people sharing the word and their faith. I hope it bring him joy to see all the people who were inspired because of their love for God and His Word.

Day Twenty-Five Journal

◊ How can you be consistent in your work for God today?

◊ What is the legacy you want "your work" to leave on this Earth?

_____

_____

_____

_____

_____

_____

_____

_____

_____

_____

_____

_____

_____

_____

_____

_____

_____

_____

Bible Journal   1 Corinthians 15   Date _____

I Thank You for

I Heard You _____

_____

_____

_____

_____

_____

I Observed

I Learned _____

_____

_____

_____

_____

_____

I Pray

Day Twenty-Six Journal

◊ Define humility in your own words and the biblical meaning.

◊ What does "passion" means in this verse?

◊ Based on this scripture, what is God's expectation of us?

_____

_____

_____

_____

_____

_____

_____

_____

_____

_____

_____

_____

_____

_____

_____

Bible Journal   James 4   Date _____

I Thank You for

I Heard You _____
_____
_____
_____
_____
_____

I Observed

I Learned _____
_____
_____
_____
_____
_____

I Pray

Day Twenty-Seven Devotional

"I lift up my eyes to the mountains— where does my help come from? My help comes from the Lord, the Maker of heaven and earth."

- Psalm 121:1-2 NIV

About 1 ½ moths into our 2nd pregnancy I went to the bathroom and found that I was bleeding. I was mortified. My first thought was this can't be seriously happening again. I literally wanted to fall on the floor, ball up, and cry. But I refused to fall apart in public, it's just not who I am. So I continued about my day.

And the bleeding continued and by my second trip to the bathroom. All I could do was look at the ceiling and begin to pray. That day I prayed to God in a way I never had before. Instead of trying to beg and plead my case or bargain for God to give me my way.

I just gave in. I told Him that whatever His will is, I'm ok with it. In my heart I felt that he had given me this second chance for a reason. But I also knew that many women experience multiple miscarriages and infertility. I reminded myself that God only wants the best for us. And I knew that if this ended in lost He was going to turn it around for my good.

In that moment, I realized I trusted Him. I knew whatever plan He had for my life it far outweigh my personal desires. I gave it over to Him. I began to think of ways that my lost could be for my good. Like maybe I was meant to foster an amazing child or to share my infertility issues with other woman who need encouragement.

I decided in that moment that whatever plan He had for me it was going to be better than what I had imagined. Now I'm entering into my 3rd trimester with baby Rose and though the fear of lost creeps in from time to time. I still have to go back to that moment in bathroom and remember the strength of God's promises that I stood on.

No matter what pain you've experience if you just remember that God is right there helping you through it. Trust the plan he has for you. The pain will pass and you will make it through the other side of the storm to the rainbow. It takes courage to trust God above our own wants, desires, and vision for our life. However, it's possible. It is beautiful. And it's a kind of peace I can't describe.

Day Twenty-Seven Journal

◊ How can you acknowledge that God is your help?

◊ Knowing that the Lord is your keeper, how does that help you move forward in this life? What does that do for you spiritually?

_____

_____

_____

_____

_____

_____

_____

_____

_____

_____

_____

_____

_____

_____

Bible Journal   Psalm 121   Date _____

I Thank You for

I Heard You _____

_____

_____

_____

_____

_____

I Observed

I Learned _____

_____

_____

_____

_____

_____

I Pray

Day Twenty-Eight Journal

◊ Why is it important to seek God's wisdom, as we go through life?

◊ How can seeking our own desires lead us to sin?

_____

_____

_____

_____

_____

_____

_____

_____

_____

_____

_____

_____

_____

_____

_____

_____

_____

_____

Bible Journal   James 1   Date _____

I Thank You for

I Heard You _____
_____
_____
_____
_____
_____

I Observed

I Learned _____
_____
_____
_____
_____
_____

I Pray

Day Twenty-Nine Devotional

"The Lord is my shepherd, I lack nothing. He makes me lie down in green pastures, he leads me beside quiet waters, he refreshes my soul."

- Psalm 23:1-2 NIV

I was about 11 years old, my mom and I were at a gas station she asked me to go in to pay for the gas. There was this group of men standing outside of the gas station. I looked at the group and back at my Mom she then told me that I didn't need to be afraid.

I can remember walking past them and mentally reciting, "Though I walk through the shadows of death." In that moment I was convinced I was walking through dangerous territory. Not even my Moms words could comfort me. The only thing I could think to do was recite the scripture I was taught. Our Sunday school teacher Ms. Annette had been working with us for about a month to memorize Psalm 23.

Although I couldn't understand the full meaning of those words back then. They still comforted me as a kid in

Compton, California. I imagined back then that Ms. Annette chose Psalm 23 for just that reason.

Because she knew, there would be moments in our lives as children and adults where we would feel alone and scared. Moreover, that we would need the words of God to confirm that we need not fear evil because he is always with us. Even today over 16 years later, I'm able to recite this verse from memory.

There have been so many moments in my life where those words have helped me, "though I walk through the shadows of death." No matter where I go, how dangerous it maybe, God is with me. Over time its affirmed my belief that God is real.

Every day we see another day is a blessing. It's only because of God that your still here. Standing strong despite the dangers, you have encounter in the world. You are living proof.

Only God can protect, guide, restore, comfort, prepare, and anoint us for the plan he has for our lives.

Day Twenty-Nine Journal

◊ How can you demonstrate courage and fearlessness when you face danger?

◊ Describe what being fearful would look like. How can you ensure you act with courage and faith?

_____

_____

_____

_____

_____

_____

_____

_____

_____

_____

_____

_____

_____

_____

_____

_____

_____

_____

_____

_____

_____

_____

_____

_____

_____

_____

_____

_____

_____

_____

_____

_____

_____

_____

_____

_____

_____

Bible Journal   Psalm 23   Date_____

I Thank You for

I Heard You _____

_____

_____

_____

_____

I Observed

I Learned _____

_____

_____

_____

_____

I Pray

Day Thirty Journal

◊ Why was it ironic for Abraham to be a "great nation"?

◊ Describe the strength of Abram faith to believe he was going to be the Father of many nations.

_____

_____

_____

_____

_____

_____

_____

_____

_____

_____

_____

_____

_____

_____

_____

_____

_____

_____

_____

_____

_____

_____

_____

_____

_____

_____

_____

_____

_____

_____

_____

_____

_____

_____

_____

_____

_____

_____

_____

_____

Bible Journal   Genesis 12   Date _____

I Thank You for

I Heard You _____

_____

_____

_____

_____

_____

I Observed

I Learned _____

_____

_____

_____

_____

_____

I Pray

Day Thirty-One Devotional

"Surely God is my salvation; I will trust and not be afraid. The Lord, the Lord himself, is my strength and my defense; he has become my salvation."

- Isaiah 12:2 NIV

God is truly amazing. And so obviously not human. I can't say enough about how thankful I am that he is such a Holy, merciful, and forgiving God.

Forgiveness is something I have surely struggled with my entire life. I'll let it go and move on but I'll never be able to forget what was done. Often times I find myself still getting upset about past experiences.

I realized that forgiveness was truly something I had to master if I wanted to be forgiven for my sins. I am constantly working and praying to be better at forgiving others. But it is surely a work in progress and so am I.

Even with Harley (our puppy) I struggle at times to forgive him when he has an accident in the house or bites me (he is playful). If Harley poops in the house and then fall down the steps, and yes this has actually happened because he's always running full speed up and down the steps. Of course, I'm going to comfort him and make sure he's not injured. But after that he's going in his cage, because I'm still not ready to forgive him for pooping in the house.

Boy am I thankful that Father God is no the same kind of parent as I am. When I need him even if I'm in the wrong he's there for me. He doesn't check my wounds and then punish me for my sins. He loves me despite my mistakes.

How He manages to gives us all that we need even when we don't deserve it. How He fiercely protects us and lifts us up even when we don't acknowledge His presences. Like how could you not love Him.

The more I learn about Him the more I adore Him simply for who He is. Instead of loving Him because of what He's done for me. He is All knowing, Kind, Caring, Loving, Generous, Holy, Protective, Encouraging, Merciful, Forgiving, and Perfect in all his ways. How could you not want to spend the rest of your eternal life praising Him.

Day Thirty-One Journal

◊   What does salvation means to you?

◊   Why is singing the Lords praises important?

_____

_____

_____

_____

_____

_____

_____

_____

_____

_____

_____

_____

_____

_____

_____

_____

Bible Journal   Isaiah 12   Date _____

I Thank You for

I Heard You _____

_____

_____

_____

_____

I Observed

I Learned _____

_____

_____

_____

_____

I Pray

Day Thirty-Two Journal

◊ What about Ruth actions was Boaz referring to when he said, "May the Lord repay you"?

◊ How can you be more like Ruth today?

_____

_____

_____

_____

_____

_____

_____

_____

_____

_____

_____

_____

_____

_____

_____

_____

_____

Bible Journal   Ruth 2   Date _____

I Thank You for

I Heard You _____

_____
_____
_____
_____
_____

I Observed

I Learned _____

_____
_____
_____
_____
_____

I Pray

Day Thirty-Three Devotional

"Humble yourselves, therefore, under God's mighty hand, that he may lift you up in due time. Cast all your anxiety on him because he cares for you."

- 1 Peter 5:6-7 NIV

Humbling myself before God was a struggle for me. I had let my ego grow out of control and I didn't think I needed to bow down to anyone or anything. Not even God. Which I can now see was a big part of my downfall.

While confidence is great when you're cocky it's not cute, becoming, or relatable. There is no telling how many people I offended because my nose was stuck in the air. No one could tell nothing. I was exuding this I am better than you are attitude. When the truth is, I really had no reason to be.

All I had was two degrees under my belt and a little bit of life experience, which amounted to nothing without faith and a strong relationship with God. I didn't have a clue about corporate America. I can tell you now that corporate America can be a shark tank. There are a lot of companies and people out there who will gladly use you up and spit you out without a second thought.

Although failure and disappointment is a part of life going through it would have been easier with God. I think back and wish I had devoted myself to prayer, church attendance, or bible reading. Something or anything that would have helped me get my life on track. Because carrying the burden of my ego, work pressure, and a personal life alone eventually lead to anxiety attacks.

Despite my ego, my career was going nowhere fast. I was demoted and at risk of a pay decrease needless to say I was stressed, unhappy, and bitter. I began to read Joel Osteen daily devotional app and it inspired me to jump start my spiritual journey. I began to pray and seek the word because I was in desperate need of direction.

The more I read the Word and prayed, I began to realize just how much I needed the Lord. This verse is one of the first verses I bookmarked and began to pray over my life. Not until I surrendered and humbled myself to the Lord, did I begin to see a glimpse of the light on the other side of the tunnel. Thank Jesus and the Lord above for being a light in my life.

Day Thirty-Three Journal

◊   Write a prayer asking God to carry your burdens.
◊   How can you exhibit humility today?

_____

_____

_____

_____

_____

_____

_____

_____

_____

_____

_____

_____

_____

_____

_____

_____

Bible Journal   1 Peter 5   Date _____

I Thank You for

I Heard You _____
_____
_____
_____
_____
_____

I Observed

I Learned _____
_____
_____
_____
_____
_____

I Pray

Day Thirty-Four Journal

◊ What is the race that has been set before us?

◊ What can you do to ensure "no bitter root grows" in your life?

_____

_____

_____

_____

_____

_____

_____

_____

_____

_____

_____

_____

_____

_____

_____

_____

_____

_____

Bible Journal   Hebrew 12   Date _____

I Thank You for

I Heard You _____
_____
_____
_____
_____
_____

I Observed

I Learned _____
_____
_____
_____
_____
_____

I Pray

Day Thirty-Five Devotional

"Not that I have already obtained all this, or have already arrived at my goal, but I press on to take hold of that for which Christ Jesus took hold of me."
- Philippians 3:12 NIV

Last year I was inspired to write my first book a faith journal. I created it because I myself needed it for my bible study and figured others might also. During this time I was actually writing a book but I felt the spirit move me toward making the faith journal the first book I released.

We have all heard the saying if you build it they will come. I built it and not as many people came as I was expecting. Within a month, I quickly realized that motto is no longer relevant for any business. I was thoroughly disappointed because I envisioned this book would transform my income.

I regularly shared it across social media and with my audience. But still nothing. My original expectation was that I would sell at least 50-100 copies per month. I tried all the strategies I had read online but I wasn't seeing the results everyone else had spoken of.

I was frustrated to say the least. But I just couldn't seem to move forward. I spent months redesigning the cover thinking it would help with sales but I just couldn't come up with a worthy design.

I originally planned to release four books in 2017 but I started to think what's the point. I couldn't stop looking back. Months were beginning to pass me by and it was like I was still standing.

We all fail from time to time. Not every great idea comes to fruition the way you imagined. But failing doesn't mean we've reached the end of the road on our journey towards redemption. You have to keep working.

Balancing faith and work is not always easy. You have to allow your failure, sins, and mistakes to fuel you forward not stop you dead in your tracks. The worst thing you can do is to soak in your failure. Instead, you have to allow your failure to spark growth, strengthen your faith, remind you of the purpose God has over your life, and move you forward toward expanding God's kingdom.

Focusing on our sins instead of repenting them and continuing to work is exactly what the devil wants. He wants you to think you're not worthy. He want you to give up the fight for God's kingdom. But you have to keep making strides towards your goals and encourage those around us to do the same. We need as many warriors as possible pushing God's kingdom forward.

Day Thirty-Five Journal

◊ What are you doing to strain forward towards your goals?

◊ Write a prayer asking that God help you continue forward when faced with failure, sin, or mistake.

_____

_____

_____

_____

_____

_____

_____

_____

_____

_____

_____

_____

_____

_____

_____

_____

_____

_____

_____

_____

_____

_____

_____

_____

_____

_____

_____

_____

_____

_____

_____

_____

_____

_____

_____

_____

_____

_____

_____

_____

_____

Bible Journal   *Philippians* 3   Date _____

I *Thank* You for

I *Heard* You _____
_____
_____
_____
_____
_____

I *Observed*

I *Learned* _____
_____
_____
_____
_____
_____

I *Pray*

Day Thirty-Six Journal

◊ Knowing that we can never hid from God. Why is it important to confess your sins? How can you use this to improve your relationship with God?

◊ Write a prayer about how thankful you are for the grace and mercy we have in Jesus.

_____

_____

_____

_____

_____

_____

_____

_____

_____

_____

_____

_____

_____

_____

_____

Bible Journal   Hebrews 4   Date_____

I Thank You for

I Heard You _____

_____

_____

_____

_____

I Observed

I Learned _____

_____

_____

_____

_____

I Pray

Day Thirty-Seven Devotional

"For no word from God will ever fail."

- Luke 1:37 NIV

Can you even begin to imagine having faith as strong as Mary? I don't know about you but if an angel told me as a virgin I was going to bear a child whom will be the Son of Man. I think would faint. But not Mary she was calm, cool, and collected. As if she knew the plans, the Lord had for her. She was ready to serve.

I feel like right now I'm in the season of getting ready. I'm trying to get ready so I can stay ready. I don't know for sure what he's called me to do. But when he calls me to do something I want to be ready to move no questions asked.

In my spiritual journey, I feel like I still have so much more to learn. Every day I feel like God shows me something new. I constantly getting inspired to write, share, and do new things. Sometimes I feel myself being pulled in 100 different directions.

One of the things I've been working on in the last month has been to focus. Focus on one thing at a time.

One lesson at a time, one book at a time, one project at a time because I want the work I do for God to be excellent.

It can be hard at times to really focus on silencing our surroundings and ourselves so that we can hear God. After all, we all have bills, jobs, and obligations so making the time to do what we feel God has called us to do and keeping up with life can be difficult. If you're like me and feel moved to do a lot of different things then it can be downright overwhelming to try and decipher your desires and God plans for you.

Ultimately, we can never be sure that we are going to get it right each time. But you have to make a decision and move forward with it. Even if it is something small like finding a church home, volunteering, or hosting a church event. God already knows the plan He has for you and He knows what you're going to do. So let's take the pressure off and just be the best servants we can be. After all it's not a competition.

Day Thirty-Seven Journal

◊ How can you prepare today to be a servant of God?

◊ What does it mean to have faith like Mary? How can you demonstrate faith like Mary?

_____

_____

_____

_____

_____

_____

_____

_____

_____

_____

_____

_____

_____

_____

_____

_____

_____

_____

Bible Journal   Luke 1:26-56   Date _____

I Thank You for

I Heard You _____
_____
_____
_____
_____

I Observed

I Learned _____
_____
_____
_____
_____

I Pray

Day Thirty-Eight Journal

◊ Write down three examples of how self-made religion (or worldly wisdom) affects today's culture.

◊ Why is it important to avoid worldly wisdom (or human traditions)?

_____

_____

_____

_____

_____

_____

_____

_____

_____

_____

_____

_____

_____

_____

_____

_____

_____

_____

_____

_____

_____

_____

_____

_____

_____

_____

_____

_____

_____

_____

_____

_____

_____

_____

_____

_____

_____

Bible Journal Colossians 2 Date _____

I Thank You for

I Heard You _____
_____
_____
_____
_____
_____

I Observed

I Learned _____
_____
_____
_____
_____
_____

I Pray

Day Thirty-Nine Devotional

"Not only so, but we also glory in our sufferings, because we know that suffering produces perseverance; perseverance, character; and character, hope."
- Romans 5:3-4 NIV

Losing our first pregnancy in June was one of the most painful experiences of my life. The timing could not have been any worst. We went to the hospital the day before our flight to California.

We were there for hours and the only people we seen was the admission nurse and sonographer. After viewing the ultrasound and seeing there was no fetus despite the fact that I was almost 9 weeks, we knew we were miscarrying. So we decided to leave the hospital without hearing it from a doctor. Plus, we were in desperate need of sleep before flying out.

I had been looking forward to this trip to California for almost a year. I don't get to go home often so when I do it's usually a special occasion. And this trip was because my cousin was getting married and expecting her first child.

How ironic.

Nonetheless, we had a great trip and a great time with our family. I think it was exactly what we needed to get our minds off our situation. The weekend was over and we headed to the airport to return to Georgia.

By the time we got pass the security checkpoint I was experiencing what felt like the worst cramps ever. It completely caught me off guard. My husband purchased ibuprofen and I took a large dose because there was no way I was going to be able to make it through a 3-hour flight with this pain.

Once we got home, the pain had intensified again. I was literally in my bed rocking back in forth thinking there is no way miscarrying should be this painful. Like I'm already emotionally in pain. But to go through this physical pain feels a bit sadistic.

I took some hydrocodone and tried to lay down. But it wasn't long before I had the urge to use the restroom. Before I knew it, there it was. I looked in the toilet and there it was, the gestational sac. My pregnancy was over.

Miscarrying did two things for me; it confirmed again that life is a precious gift and that as quickly as life can be given it can be taken. Because I miscarried I try so hard to savor every moment of my second pregnancy. I constantly pray and thank God for our little one.

The pains I experienced emotionally and physically was given purpose the moment baby Rose entered our lives. We truly can endure all things with Christ who strengthens us. Suffering brings us closer to Christ.

I know it's not always easy to see during tough times. But even our sufferings has a purpose. This verses helped strengthen the trust I have in God's plan.

Day Thirty-Nine Journal

◊ Write a prayer that will serve as you reminder of this verse during tough times.

◊ Challenge yourself and try to find the purpose in a recent lost. How that experience shaped you and your faith?

_____

_____

_____

_____

_____

_____

_____

_____

_____

_____

_____

_____

_____

_____

_____

Bible Journal   *Romans* 5   Date _____

I *Thank* You for

I *Heard* You _____

_____

_____

_____

_____

I *Observed*

I *Learned* _____

_____

_____

_____

_____

I *Pray*

Day Forty Journal

◊ What can you do to be a light in this world?

◊ How can you by living a life according to God's wisdom expose those who live in darkness?

_____

_____

_____

_____

_____

_____

_____

_____

_____

_____

_____

_____

_____

_____

_____

_____

_____

_____

_____

_____

_____

_____

_____

_____

_____

_____

_____

_____

_____

_____

_____

_____

_____

_____

_____

_____

_____

_____

_____

Bible Journal   Ephesians 5   Date _____

I Thank You for

I Heard You _____

_____
_____
_____
_____

I Observed

I Learned _____

_____
_____
_____
_____

I Pray

Day Forty-One Devotional

"Ask and it will be given to you; seek and you will find; knock and the door will be opened to you."

- Matthew 7:7 NIV

The first time I heard this statement was actually on "The Secret" movie, which talks about how you can unlock your full potential and power. Of course, it wasn't stated as an excerpt from the Bible. But as a proclamation of how each individual has the ability to change their life with this simple premise of Ask, Seek, and Knock.

Needless to say I was pumped after I watched this video like so many other viewers. I created a vision board as suggested and set out to make my dreams a reality. But as you probably already guess life is not that simple and if it was wouldn't we all be a success story.

Yes there is power in the tongue. But we must do more than speak of the things we would like to see happen in our life. Our heart, actions, and thoughts must align with the word in order to begin to understand our roles in fulfilling God's purpose for our lives.

Moral of the story this verse is not about God being a genie that will appear from a magic lamp to grant our every wish at the drop of a dime. But it is an effort to acknowledge that he hears us. And to reinforce that our prayers and efforts will be answered in His time.

I'm so thank that I began to read Matthews shortly after watching "The Secret." The book of Matthews helped me to understand that ask, seek, and knock is more about having faith, trusting in the Lord, and persistently seeking Him.

Come to God and ask humbly for the fulfillment of your needs. Understanding that He is already fully aware. The gesture of asking is about acknowledging that you need Him to provide for you.

Come to God in prayer and seek Him. Seek Him and His will consistently and whole-heartedly, understanding that you don't know the plans He has for you. But trusting that His plan is better than your own. Praying that His will prevails over your desires.

Come to God persistently and patiently knocking for His intervention. Even when you don't see things changing. Stay continuous in your prayers. Remain confident in His abilities and will.

Day Forty-One Journal

◊ How can you incorporate ask, seek, and knock into your prayer life today?

◊ What can you do to ensure you treat others the way you want to be treated?

_____

_____

_____

_____

_____

_____

_____

_____

_____

_____

_____

_____

_____

_____

_____

_____

Bible Journal   Matthews 7   Date _____

I Thank You for

I Heard You _____

_____

_____

_____

_____

_____

I Observed

I Learned _____

_____

_____

_____

_____

_____

I Pray

Day Forty-Two Journal

◊ Why is it important to call upon the Lord?
◊ What does "I know the plans I have for you" mean to you?

_____

_____

_____

_____

_____

_____

_____

_____

_____

_____

_____

_____

_____

_____

_____

_____

_____

_____

_____

_____

_____

_____

_____

_____

_____

_____

_____

_____

_____

_____

_____

_____

_____

_____

_____

_____

_____

Bible Journal   Jeremiah 29   Date _____

I Thank You for

I Heard You _____

_____

_____

_____

_____

_____

I Observed

I Learned _____

_____

_____

_____

_____

I Pray

Day Forty-Three Journal

◊ How can we as Christians glorify the Lord "with one voice"?

◊ How can you be more welcoming today?

_____

_____

_____

_____

_____

_____

_____

_____

_____

_____

_____

_____

_____

_____

_____

_____

_____

_____

_____

_____

_____

_____

_____

_____

_____

_____

_____

_____

_____

_____

_____

_____

_____

_____

_____

_____

_____

_____

Bible Journal   Romans 15   Date _____

I Thank You for

I Heard You _____

_____

_____

_____

_____

I Observed

I Learned _____

_____

_____

_____

_____

I Pray

Day Forty-Four Journal

◊ Why is love important as a Christian?

◊ How can you become a more loving person?

_____

_____

_____

_____

_____

_____

_____

_____

_____

_____

_____

_____

_____

_____

_____

_____

_____

_____

_____

Bible Journal   1 Corinthians 13   Date _____

I Thank You for

I Heard You _____

_____

_____

_____

_____

I Observed

I Learned _____

_____

_____

_____

_____

I Pray

Day Forty-Five Journal

◊ How can you show God that you are willing to wait on Him?

◊ Write a prayer acknowledging your thankfulness that even in our sins God still grants us hope and mercy.

_____

_____

_____

_____

_____

_____

_____

_____

_____

_____

_____

_____

_____

_____

_____

_____

_____

_____

Bible Journal   Lamentations 3   Date _____

I Thank You for

I Heard You _____

_____

_____

_____

_____

I Observed

I Learned _____

_____

_____

_____

_____

I Pray

ABOUT THE AUTHOR

ChellBee is a daughter of Christ, wife, and obsessive planner. Her passion for writing drove her to create a blog where she empowers women to embrace there imperfect journey. But along the way, she realized she would be doing a disservice if she failed to share how importance my faith has been throughout my journey.

Creating and maintaining a lasting relationship with God is not always easy but with commitment, consistency, and the right tools its possible. She wanted to help women like her with all the above.

ChellBee grew up in the inner city of Compton, California, with her two sisters and mother. When she was 12, her family uprooted to the suburbs of Atlanta, GA where she later attended college.

ChellBee grew up in the inner city of Compton, California, with her two sisters and mother. When she was 12, her family uprooted to the suburbs of Atlanta, GA where she later attended college.

From a young age, she enjoyed writing in many different forms, from poetry and songs, to short story telling. Throughout her life writing allowed her to overcome the many personal obstacles she have faced.

Find more of ChellBee

Facebook: ChellBee
Instagram: @iamChellBee
Twitter: @iamChellBee
YouTube: Chell Bee
www.ChellBee.com

Made in the USA
Columbia, SC
13 August 2023